Clara Barton
Angel of the Battlefield

Colleen Adams

Rosen
REAL
READERS

The Rosen Publishing Group, Inc.
New York

Published in 2002 by The Rosen Publishing Group, Inc.
29 East 21st Street, New York, NY 10010

Book Design: Ron A. Churley

Photo Credits: Cover, p. 1 © PhotoWorld/FPG International; pp. 5, 9, 13 © National Park Service, Clara Barton National Historic Site; pp. 7, 11, 14 © The Granger Collection, New York.

ISBN: 0-8239-8214-9
6-pack ISBN: 0-8239-8617-9

Manufactured in the United States of America

Contents

Clara's Early Years

Clara Barton was born in Oxford, Massachusetts, on December 25, 1821. Clara was the youngest of five children. She was a quiet, shy child who liked school. Clara loved helping other people.

This is the earliest known photograph of Clara Barton. It was taken sometime between 1850 and 1851.

Clara's Jobs

Clara began teaching when she was seventeen. She helped many children during the ten years she spent as a teacher. Clara decided she wanted to learn new things and took a job in Washington, D.C. She became the first woman to work as a clerk in a government office.

Clara had many different jobs during her lifetime.

The Civil War

In 1861, Clara quit her job to work as a nurse during the **American Civil War**. Clara wanted to take food and **medicine** directly to the **soldiers**. She asked the United States government to allow her to go to the **battlefield**.

Clara collected food, clothing, and other supplies to take to the battlefield.

8

9

Angel of the Battlefield

A few months later, Clara was the first woman allowed to go to the battlefield. She cleaned soldiers' **wounds** and changed their **bandages**. Clara was always very kind to the soldiers. They called her the "Angel of the Battlefield."

Clara helped doctors take care of sick and wounded soldiers.

Life After the War

After the war, the government put Clara in charge of a search for missing soldiers. She also fought for women's rights and the rights of African Americans. Later, Clara stayed in Europe (YER-up) to work with a group called the Red Cross. This group helped give supplies and medical aid to soldiers all over the world.

Clara started the first Red Cross in the United States in 1881.

13

The American Red Cross

Clara started the first Red Cross in the United States to help people during times of war and peace. This group also helped people who lived in places that had been destroyed by floods, fires, and storms. Today, the Red Cross continues Clara Barton's work by offering help and **services** for all people.

Glossary

American Civil War A war between the Northern and Southern states of the United States from 1861 to 1865.

bandage A strip of cloth used to wrap or cover a cut on the body.

battlefield The place where a war is fought or has been fought.

medicine A drug that is used to prevent or treat a sickness.

service Something that a person does to help someone else.

soldier A member of an army.

wound A torn or cut place on the body.

Index